2001 JOHN W. HOLMES MEMORIAL LECTURE

Global Governance and the Changing Face of International Law

By Charlotte Ku

Executive Director,
American Society of International Law (ASIL)
and Former Chair,
ACUNS Board of Directors

*Prepared for Delivery at the Annual Meeting of the
Academic Council on the United Nations System
June 16-18, 2001, Puebla, Mexico*

ACUNS REPORTS & PAPERS
2001 No.2

ABOUT THE JOHN W. HOLMES MEMORIAL LECTURE SERIES

The Academic Council on the United Nations System inaugurated the John W. Holmes Memorial Lecture Series in 1989 in honor of a founding member of ACUNS. Mr. Holmes had served on the planning committee for the founding conference of ACUNS and the provisional committee in 1987-88. The talk he prepared for the first ACUNS Annual Meeting in 1988, *Looking Backwards and Forwards*, was the first publication in the Councilís series of Reports and Papers.

John W. Holmes joined the Canadian Department of External Affairs in 1943 and participated in the planning of the United Nations. He attended the preparatory commission in 1945 and the first session of the General Assembly, and later served as head of UN Affairs in Ottawa and as Under-Secretary of the Department of External Affairs. In 1960, he left public service for a second career in teaching and scholarship, basing himself at the Canadian Institute of International Affairs and the University of Toronto.

Mr. Holmes brought to the Academic Council a lifetime of experience and reflection on international politics and the role of the United Nations. He also brought a marvelous mix of idealism and realism, a mix that showed up clearly in the report, *Looking Backwards and Forwards*. In the conclusion, he spoke of the need for reexamining the role of the UN in a way that captures the basic purposes of the Academic Council. It is an ideal time, he said, to launch in all our countries that renewed examination of past experience of the UN, to discover on what we can build and where not to venture, how we can use the growing threat to the globe itself to create the will for international self-discipline which is what international institutions are all about.

Contents

1. Perceptions of International Law   1

2. Growth of International Law   2

3. Functions and Modalities of International Law   5

4. The Voluntarist Period *(begins circa 1648)*   8

5. The Institutionalist Period *(begins circa 1899)*   14

6. The Civil Society Period *(begins circa 1975)*   26

7. Conclusion   36

To the memory of
Harold K. Jacobson with gratitude

Global Governance and the Changing Face of International Law

1. PERCEPTIONS OF INTERNATIONAL LAW

Adaptation, flexibility and change are not words that many seem to associate with international law. As a result, the proposition that international law is a factor for change in international affairs appears unrealistic. But I would like to take the opportunity of this Holmes Lecture to tell you why I believe international law is a factor for adaptation and change in international relations, and how I see it remaining as a factor in global governance into the future.

Two of the more persistent criticisms leveled at international law are that:

1. it is a utopian system that does not take into account power and politics; and

2. that it is static and not relevant to world affairs.

Examples exist to justify these criticisms. Focusing on specific shortcomings, however, misses the dynamism of international law. Although the space of a lecture does not allow a comprehensive examination of how international law has changed to meet new situations, I hope that insight into how it works, how it has addressed power, and how it has adapted might provide a deeper understanding of how to assess its performance, utility, and relevance to issues of global governance.

I propose to do this by looking at three periods that encompass the development of several significant features of contemporary international life. The three periods are:

I. The Voluntarist Period *(begins circa 1648)*

II. The Institutionalist Period *(begins circa 1899)*

III. The Civil Society Period *(begins circa 1975)*

Each of these periods highlights a particular development and demonstrates how international law has adapted to changing conditions by drawing from the experience of one period to build the next. The implications of these developments for shaping future values and community will also be considered. I identify only a starting point to the periods because significant features of each period remain with us today. The periods and their features overlap and interact.

2. GROWTH OF INTERNATIONAL LAW

In its most basic form, international law is recognized as a body of rules and practices that regulates state behavior in the conduct of international relations. But, in the three and a half centuries since modern international law's establishment in international relations, much has changed. Christian Wiktor's chronological presentation of all multilateral treaties from 1648 to 1995 shows the changes in the subject matter of multilateral treaties. We find the first non-political or non-military treaty in this collection in 1691 — the Provisional Convention Regarding Commerce and Navigation in France — with the next appearing in 1815 — Rules Concerning the Navigation of the Rhine River, followed by the Convention Relative to Navigation of the Elbe in 1822.

From 1850 to the present, the number of treaties and treaty subjects has mushroomed. First, let us take a look at the subject matter of treaties. Table 1 organizes multilateral treaties into general treaty subjects. These subject listings represent a simplification of the more than 250 subject headings used by the United Nations to classify treaties. The seven categories are: political/diplomatic, military, economic, human welfare, cultural, environment and other.

TABLE 1: MULTILATERAL TREATY SUBJECTS BY PERIOD[1]
1648-1995*

	1648-1750		1751-1850		1851-1899		1900-1925		1926-1950		1951-1975		1976-1995	
	#	%	#	%	#	%	#	%	#	%	#	%	#	%
Political/ Diplomatic	72	84%	64	64%	162	48%	249	38%	292	25%	508	25%	315	19%
Military	13	18%	8	8%	17	8%	55	8%	99	8%	80	4%	59	4%
Economic	1	1%	13	13%	143	42%	241	36%	546	46%	885	43%	719	44%
Human Welfare			13	13%	11	3%	68	10%	144	12%	158	8%	111	7%
Cultural			1	1%			7	1%	17	1%	34	2%	24	1%
Environment			1	1%	3	.8%	20	3%	56	5%	134	7%	209	13%
Other					2	.6%	23	3%	29	2%	248	12%	182	11%
Period Total	86	100%	100	100%	338	100%	663	100%	1,183	100%	2,047	100%	1,619	100%

* Time periods were selected to balance natural chronological breaks and adequate amounts of data for each period so that conclusions are reasonable.

In addition to the change in subject matter, it is important to keep in mind the large increase in multilateral treaty activity over these several hundred years. Compare the fact that there were 86 multilateral treaties for the first 100 years of this collection to the more than 2,000 multilateral treaties for the 25 year period between 1951 and 1975. The data also show a drop-off in the number of new multilateral treaties being concluded in the last period covered — 1976-1995.

It may also be helpful to understand that of the 6,000 multilateral treaties, only 30% are general multilateral treaties, that is, open to all states for participation. Seventy percent are plurilateral treaties that are limited in participation by geographic region or by subject matter. Explosive as these numbers are, multilateral treaties are only 10% of all treaty activity in the world. The bulk of international activity and international law remains on a bilateral basis. And treaties themselves are only one form of expressing transnational activity that also includes informal arrangements and practices.

3. FUNCTIONS AND MODALITIES OF INTERNATIONAL LAW

The level of international interaction as expressed through treaty activity has created a more complex and interwoven system of legal relationships. Fundamentally, international law serves the purpose, as a factor in ordering international relations, of managing by systemic change and adaptation the conflict generated by power and politics. Treaties are a tool used for this purpose and an expression of the political solutions arrived at. Thus, to the extent that E.H. Carr was critical of those who conceived of international law as divorced from politics, he was right. He wrote:

> Every system of law presupposes an initial political decision, whether explicit or implied, whether achieved by voting or by bargaining or by force, as to the authority entitled to make and unmake law. Behind all law there is this necessary political background. The ultimate authority of law derives from politics.[2]

Effective operation of the law, international or otherwise, requires that three elements be in alignment:

* a legal concept that is developed enough to be communicated clearly;

* a structure or framework that can support the operation of the law; and

* the political consensus and will of the system's members to use the law.

Where law has failed, its failure can be traced to the absence of one of these elements.

International law provides the framework for political discourse among members of the international system. The framework does not guarantee consensus, but it does foster the ongoing discourse and participation needed to provide conceptual clarity in developing legal obligations and gaining their acceptance. In playing this role, international law performs two different functions — one is to provide a framework for cross border interactions, and another is to shape the values and goals these interactions are pursuing. Paul Diehl and I have called the first set of functions the *"operating system"* of international law, and

the second set the *"normative system."*[3] Critics of international
law perceive its failure because of their expectation that
international law will change a particular behavior or solve a
specific problem, even though the international legal framework
may sustain the political discourse and interaction that
eventually leads to a solution.

International law today has moved towards acknowledging that
there are some forms of behavior that are so repugnant to global
order that they are generally proscribed. These *jus cogens* norms
emphasize the protection of human dignity and ban such
practices as slavery, torture, and genocide. Thus, the separation
between the operating and the normative may not always be
clear. Understanding the relationship between the two is
further complicated by the volume of interactions that
constitutes international relations today.

If there is an enduring theme to international relations, it is one
of expansion and diffusion — both in the number of actors and
in the number of subject matters dealt with at the interstate
level. This has in turn led to a diffusion of power among the
actors in the system, although not necessarily a diminution of
each actor's power. How well international law has expanded
its framework to address this diffusion is a key test of
international law's relevance to global governance questions in
the future. The track record as I see it is a strong one, and I
would now like to turn to the three periods (the voluntarist, the
institutionalist, and the civil society) to support this
observation.

4. THE VOLUNTARIST PERIOD *(begins circa 1648)*

Although the sovereignty and the independence of states are now so well established that it is hard to imagine a time without them, it is useful to recall that other forms of governance were available to structure the global order of the 17th century. As Hendrik Spruyt described, the state emerged from "a particular conjuncture of social and political interests in Europe."[4] This conjuncture itself was the product of the structured interactions and political environment of the European Middle Ages.[5] State practice then developed the concept of sovereignty as the basis for self-regulated and independent action.[6] I call this period "voluntarist," because during this period states were obligated to do very little beyond what they specifically accepted.

The Peace of Westphalia in 1648 gave expression to these interests and provided the basis for the development of the state system. The Peace of Westphalia that ended the Thirty Years' War created certain assumptions, for both modern international relations and law. These are based on the existence of independent states that are:

* sovereign within their own territories,

* equal to one another,

* not answerable to any higher external authority, and

* not bound without their consent.

Translated into twentieth century terms, these assumptions can be found in the United Nations Charter in the concepts of territorial integrity and non-interference in internal affairs. These external characteristics grew out of a need for internal cohesion and governance to support economic activity and growing populations. Although Westphalia concentrated power within states, it also diffused power externally by making states answerable to no higher authority than themselves.[7]

The Peace of Westphalia not only addressed the privileges of state power, but also provided for the ongoing responsibility of the victor states, Sweden and France, to "ensure that the privileges and immunities conferred on the Princes and the free cities of Germany in the treaty shall be upheld and maintained."[8] As part of the Peace of Westphalia, the Treaty of Muenster provided for peaceful settlement of disputes through forms of arbitration or mediation, obligated parties to a cooling off period of three years prior to initiating hostilities in case of a dispute, and called for sanctions if these conditions were not fulfilled. As a stepping stone to current international legal practices, these were significant developments. The consensus that the Peace of Westphalia was the cornerstone of contemporary international law results from the enduring relevance of the procedures it established.

The Peace of Westphalia also marked the end of the hierarchy that flowed from the temporal authority of the pope and the Catholic Church. This paved the way for a system of international relations open to any state willing and able to discharge obligations for the general maintenance of orderly international relations.[9] A system of coexisting, coequal political units was created without regard to religion or form of government - republics as well as monarchies were accepted as long as they followed the precepts of the Westphalian system of international relations. Certain institutional features tied to territory were required to carry out these precepts. These features included effective control of a defined territory and population and a government capable of discharging international obligations. Under these conditions, republics like the Dutch Republic and eventually the United States joined the system.

In breaking its ties to the religious teachings of the Catholic Church, this new "secularized" international law focused on the development of state values and gave prominence to the liberty of states. It supported the operation of a voluntarist approach based on individual state consent and the balance of power. To the extent that states functioned within a common set of values, they did so principally within a framework of self-preservation. Law functioned through rather than above states, and state consent was key to the undertaking of any legal obligation. Classic expression of this understanding is found in the decision of the Permanent Court of International Justice in the 1927 *Case of the S.S. Lotus* (France v. Turkey):

> International law governs relations between independent States. The rules of law binding upon States therefore emanate from their own free will as expressed in conventions or by usages generally accepted as expressing principles of law and established in order to regulate the relations between these co-existing independent

communities or with a view to the achievement of common aims. *Restrictions upon the independence of States cannot therefore be presumed.*[10]

Evaluating The Voluntarist Legacy

The practice of this period is the legacy of what Louis Henkin called *"state values,"*[11] such as territorial integrity, equality of states, and protection from external interference. In the voluntarist period, states and sovereigns were the principal actors, and the primary concern of international law was the preservation of the elements of power for the state as the primary unit of international relations. The voluntarist period contributed substantially to international law's operating system by laying the groundwork for state independence and responsibility. This led to the formalization of elements of international law's operating system that we recognize today as encompassing sovereign immunity, the law of armed conflict, alliances and treaty-based relations. The voluntarist period was one of state or sovereign consent, in which the capacity to project military power was the ultimate means of addressing and resolving conflict. The state had the capacity both to preserve order and to create disorder.[12]

Developments in this period were chiefly of an operating character since those were the needs of the system. The Industrial Revolution had not yet given rise to the modern technologies of power projection. States developed few universal norms, in part because there were few transnational problems, and the potential destruction that unfettered state power could unleash was not fully realized until the 20th century. By then, the state's capacity to destroy was covered by a veil of sovereignty to shield itself from external scrutiny. In a celebrated note entitled, "Away with the 'S' Word," written when he was president of the American Society of International Law, Louis Henkin observed that:

> Sovereignty sometimes subsumes-and conceals-important values. It is used to express the essential quality of a state, the basic entity, abstract but real, of the international political system. "Sovereignty" is used to describe the autonomy of states and the need for state consent to make law and build institutions. "Sovereignty" is used to justify and define the "privacy" of states, their political independence and territorial integrity; their right and the rights of their people to be let alone and to go their own way.

> But sovereignty has also grown a mythology of state grandeur and aggrandizement that misconceives the concept and clouds what is authentic and worthy in it, a mythology that is often empty and sometimes destructive of human values.[13]

Much as technological advances and economic interests had contributed to the formation of the state itself in the 17th and 18th centuries, so too the advances and interests of the 19th and early 20th centuries indicated the inadequacy of the territorially defined state to address them. By the mid-20th century, the advantages of cooperation outweighed the advantages of autonomy, and states were willing to strike "*sovereignty bargains*," such as the integration of important state functions in the European Union.[14] More than a century before,

European states had already recognized the cooperative and joint management of resources like rivers as an interest worth curbing their independence. As an operating system, international law provided them a framework within which to pursue these goals.

The voluntarist period acknowledged power in international relations by accepting it and by not seeking to ban the use of force in pursuit of state goals. Two factors, however, created an impetus for change:

1. The increase in the destructive capacity of states already in evidence in the 19th century.

2. A tentative but emerging international political consensus to seek an alternative to the voluntarist approach that was held responsible for the devastation that World War I brought to Europe.

In an effort to restrain the unfettered freedom of states to destroy themselves and their citizens, political leaders in the wake of World War I sought alternative approaches to managing power and conflict. This led to the creation of the security structures first of the League of Nations and then of the United Nations. The League and the UN were to be more than alliances. They were to be multipurpose institutions that could prevent conflict by providing for a range of techniques for the peaceful settlement of disputes. They were to facilitate a collective response to any unilateral attack on a member state. And they were mandated to address the economic and social roots of conflict as a means of preventing it.

As the state had emerged from the confluence of several political streams, the fashioning of the institutionalist image also grew out of the convergence of what Inis Claude called objective and subjective conditions. The objective conditions were ones of independent units interacting across borders. The subjective conditions were an awareness of shared problems and the desire to create means to manage them.[15] The subjective conditions converged in the early 20th century with an exponential increase in a state's capacity to destroy. These forces came together to convince statesmen and academics alike of the necessity for alternatives to the voluntarist approach.

5. THE INSTITUTIONALIST PERIOD *(begins circa 1899)*

The 19th century ended with the First Hague Peace Conference in 1899, called to restrict the damage that states could inflict on each other's populations by outlawing particular kinds of weapons (poison gas and exploding bullets are examples) and to limit the arms race. This approach recognized that certain problems were general in character and required the cooperation of all powers, whether large or small. It further recognized that there were problems that required long-term attention, including a need to restrain the freedom of states to wage war on each other. The Hague system therefore introduced the concept of general long-term commitments by all states — not just important states — to restrict their behavior in order to ensure self-preservation. It also moved to institutionalize alternatives to military force to resolve conflicts and introduced the idea of international legal institutions to serve that purpose. A system of public law arbitration that still exists today is a legacy of the Hague conferences of 1899 and 1907.

As the Peace of Westphalia recognized new actors in international relations, the Covenant of the League of Nations took steps to curb the freedom of states to use force at will and empowered a collective entity composed of states to call states to action when needed. As the events that led to World War II unfolded and the League of Nations was seen as incapable of addressing the challenges posed by aggressor states which had either withdrawn or been expelled from League membership, Anglo-American proposals for international institutions and law as means to resolve conflicts acquired an increasingly utopian character that looked further and further removed from power and reality.

Carr noted in *The Twenty Years' Crisis* that: "Since 1919, natural law has resumed its sway, and theories of international law have become more markedly utopian than at any previous time."[16] Traumatized by the western front and ignoring the power that lay behind their own successful domestic legal institutions, proponents of such theories crafted institutional frameworks for the peaceful settlement of disputes, when the real problem was the existence of states determined to use military force to pursue their interests.

The heart of the League's security guarantee was in Article 10 of the Covenant. It provided that: "The Members of the League undertake to respect and preserve as against external aggression the territorial integrity and existing political independence of all Members of the League." If a member were attacked, the League Council was authorized (not obligated) to call on League members to undertake an appropriate response. The deterrent character of the response depended on League members acting collectively and automatically when a violation occurred. As history demonstrated and as Carr noted, the voluntarist assumptions of international relations were far from replaced by this institutionalist approach.

No matter what the League Covenant required, states turned out to be unwilling to act other than on their own behalf. The inability of the entire League membership to act as a unit put it at a disadvantage when challenged by such politically determined and militarily strong powers as Germany and Japan in the pursuit of their interests. Stark realization of the League's ineffectiveness as a security system came when Poland invoked its alliance with France and Britain for help, not Article 10 of the Covenant, after its invasion by Germany in September 1939.

Article 10 was meant to deter, and provisions for dispute settlement were made elsewhere — in Articles 13 and 15. The League of Nations Covenant provided for arbitration and the judicial settlement of disputes, including the setting up of the Permanent Court of International Justice. If states chose not to use either of these methods for settling disputes, the Covenant required that the dispute be brought to the League Council, where the dispute might be examined and addressed before the disputing parties went to war. Failure to do so was supposed to bring about sanctions on the violator, but the League's inability to contain and to reverse aggression, despite its efforts to impose sanctions, discredited both international law and the League as an institution that could provide any meaningful security guarantees to its members.

Proponents of international law had placed their faith in Article 19 of the League Covenant, which provided:

> The Assembly may from time to time advise the reconsideration by members of the League of treaties which have become inapplicable and the consideration of international conditions whose continuance might endanger the peace of the world.

Pitman Potter explained that the motivation for Article 19 was to allow for "a periodic revision of obsolete treaties and of international situations dangerous to peace" in order to "provide a means of correcting mistakes which might be made at the time and to provide for changes of conditions with the passage of time."[17]

Although the idea may have seemed sound to those drafting Article 19, the political conditions within which Article 19 had to operate made it impossible for reliance on this provision to produce results.[18] The concern that Article 19 would be used to unravel the Versailles political settlement that accompanied the creation of the League effectively denied to all members this means for incremental change.[19] Recalling the three elements that must be kept in alignment for effective legal developments to occur (clarity of the norm, structure through which to implement the norm, and the political consensus and will to use it), Article 19 failed to achieve the necessary political consensus among states to make it work.

Despite the League of Nations' failure to deter Axis aggression, the experiment in international cooperation through international institutions was not completely discredited. On the contrary, much of what the League initiated was continued by the United Nations, which took over the League's facilities and assets. The United Nations' permanent secretariat and headquarters were modeled on the League. The International Court of Justice continued the operations of the Permanent Court of International Justice. Both the League and the UN coordinated ambitious postwar economic assistance and recovery programs.

The United Nations was established to avoid the weaknesses of the League of Nations that had caused it to fail to address effectively the power and state interests of the interwar period. Although based on the principle of sovereign equality, the UN Charter conferred a particular responsibility for maintaining peace and security on the major powers (China, the United Kingdom, the United States, the Soviet Union, and France) that collectively had defeated the Axis powers. The special status and responsibility of these powers were confirmed by their permanent membership on the United Nations Security Council.

The operating assumptions of the voluntarist period were therefore incorporated in the UN system in the role of the major powers. The UN's founders accepted that without at least the tacit consent of the major powers, it would be futile for the institution to attempt to address threats to peace. They also accepted that action against one of the major powers was unlikely to be effective and therefore should not be attempted — the veto in the Security Council for permanent members was designed to protect the UN from exceeding its capacity for effective action. Despite this recognition of power realities, aspects of the United Nations security apparatus were still unworkable in the political context of the Cold War. The earmarking of troops, for example, for use in United Nations operations (as provided by Article 43 of the UN Charter) never materialized.

Evaluating the Institutionalist Legacy

By attempting to distance law from politics and to use law in the League while disregarding state power and interests, proponents of law fell into the utopian trap that Carr described. The UN Charter has avoided this trap by acknowledging differences in power through the permanent member structure of the Security Council. However, the UN is having a hard time adjusting a system based on post-World War II assumptions about which states could, and therefore should, carry the larger responsibility for conflict prevention and resolution to one that may reflect more accurately the power of states today. But, by joining law and power and focusing on international law as a framework and as a process, the UN has realized a much more dynamic and realistic concept of the operation of law.

States themselves have promoted change within the institutionalist framework. A dramatic example can be seen in decolonization. We might consider the First Hague Peace Conference in 1899, where 26 states were represented, as a baseline. At the Second Hague Peace Conference in 1907, 44 states were represented. The United Nations today has 189 members. The numbers are even more impressive if considered in terms of people. Harold Jacobson observed that, in 1945, "almost one quarter of the world's population lived in dependent territories. By 1970 less than 1 percent of the world's population inhabited territories that had not attained self-rule, and by 1983 the number had been reduced to just over two-tenths of 1 percent."[20]

Geographically, the wave of independence started in the 18th century in North America, then spread in the 19th century to Latin America, and in the 20th century to the Middle East, Asia, Africa, and, most recently after the Cold War, to the former Soviet Union. As Jacobson concluded, decolonization resulted in a "significant restructuring of the global political system, and this restructuring has been achieved with remarkably little violence."[21]

Decolonization was all the more remarkable because there was neither legal basis nor precedent for it. It just gained a form of legal momentum propelled by state interests and economic necessity that began in the 1950s as a moral stand and within twenty years was accepted as "obligatory to bring forward dependent peoples to independence if they so chose, even though Article 73 had spoken only of self-government."[22]

As a result of decades of interaction in multilateral frameworks, the forms of law themselves have changed. This is expressed in the growing body of United Nations law and the new political/legal environment created by practices of international organizations. Oscar Schachter noted that: "UN political bodies — though denied legislative power — could act like legislatures by adopting law-making treaties and declarations of law."[23]

Though states remain the principal law-making authority, increasingly they work through frameworks provided by international institutions. Recognition and reliance on venues like the UN General Assembly mean that debates held in such organs themselves may become part of the law-making process. Substantively, contemporary issues that require a universal approach may be more readily addressed in such general forums like the organs of the United Nations or at UN sponsored worldwide conferences. Jonathan Charney concluded that "[t]he augmented role of multilateral forums in devising, launching, refining and promoting general international law has provided the international community with a more formal lawmaking process that is used often."[24]

Another form of institutional influence is seen in the role played by the UN secretariat in moving a statute for the International Criminal Court to completion. This is an example of how the intergovernmental and multilateral treaty-making process under UN sponsorship provides opportunity for influence by skilled staff carrying out the intricate coordination and drafting tasks required for preparation of such major agreements.[25]

And as members of the Academic Council on the United Nations System are certainly aware, international institutions themselves are not frozen in time and have life cycles, including a surprisingly high mortality rate.[26] For example, one-third of international governmental organizations operating in 1981 no longer existed in 1992. The growth in the number of international institutions is also not an incremental one, but rather one that "occasionally plateau[s] following periodic organizing bursts."[27]

Table 2 shows the number of multilateral treaties that created an international organization. It also shows the number of multilateral treaties that addresses some aspect of an international organization other than to create it. The growth spurts can be seen in the number of treaties that create international organizations. However, it is interesting to note that even the increased numbers represent only a modest portion of overall treaty activity.

TABLE 2:
MULTILATERAL TREATIES AND
INTERNATIONAL ORGANIZATIONS
1648-1995

Time Period	Total # of Treaties	Breakdown Number	Percent of Total
1648-1750	86	No link: 86	100%
1751-1850	100	No link:100	100%
1851-1899	338	No link: 324 Creates an IO: 3 Some link to an IO: 11	96 % 1 % 3 %
1900-1925	663	No link: 588 Creates an IO: 30 Some link to an IO: 3	91 % 5 % 4 %
1926-1950	1183	No link: 1001 Creates an IO: 58 Some link to an IO: 44	91 % 5 % 4 %
1951-1975	2047	No link: 158 Creates an IO: 165 Some link to an IO: 253	79 % 8 % 13 %
1976-1995	1619	No link: 1459 Creates an IO: 100 Some link to an IO: 60	90 % 6 % 4 %

A census of international institutions tells us that at the end of the 20th century "there are more than 250 conventional international governmental organizations (IGOs), more than 1500 other international bodies and roughly 3700 other institutions of special types, making a total of almost 5500."[28] In 1998, the UN registered 1,528 nongovernmental organizations, 40% of which were based in the United States. Despite this seeming dominance by the United States, it is less than what it had been a decade before.

Such a large number of institutions and level of activity have not left the political landscape untouched; international institutions have made their mark on law making today. They have done so not only by increasing the number of state actors through decolonization and by providing the possibility of participation by nongovernmental organizations, but also by carving out a legal status of their own. This was given expression in the International Court of Justice's 1949 *Advisory Opinion on the Reparation for Injuries Suffered in the Service of the United Nations* in which the Court acknowledged that the United Nations "possess[ed]...a large measure of international personality and the capacity to operate upon an international plane."[29]

And finally, international institutions have expanded the international political space to allow for the protection and participation of private associations and individuals in areas of international activity. Most prominent examples of this development are the European Union and the European Court of Human Rights. In the case of the European Union, Anne-Marie Slaughter and Walter Mattli wrote:

> Until 1963 the enforcement of the Rome treaty, like that of any other international treaty, depended entirely on action by the national legislatures of the member states of the community. By 1965, a citizen of a community country could ask a national court to invalidate any provision of domestic law found to conflict with certain directly applicable provisions of the treaty. By 1975, a citizen of an EC country could seek the invalidation of national law found to conflict with self-executing provisions of community secondary legislation, the "directives" to national governments passed by the EC Council of Ministers. And by 1990, community citizens could ask their national courts to interpret national legislation consistently with community legislation in the face of undue delay in passing directives on the part of national legislatures.[30]

This development, together with the pathbreaking rights provided individuals in the European Convention on Human Rights through rulings of the European Court of Human Rights, has given individuals a status and a role in the international system, including rights of action against states (including their own). Some of the likely familiar names that comprise the landmark jurisprudence of the European Court of Human Rights include *Lawless* (1961)[31] and the *Belgian Linguistic Case* (1968).[32] International institutions therefore proved not only to be the vehicle for the appearance of more than 100 new states through decolonization, but also became the growing medium for establishing the rights of private individuals and associations, both in international public discourse and increasingly in the law-making arena.

An apt segue into our third and final period comes from UN Secretary-General Kofi Annan's reflection on the UN's role in the 21st century entitled, *We the Peoples.* In the opening pages of this statement prepared for the Millennium Summit, he wrote that: "We must also adapt international institutions, through which states govern together, to the realities of the new era. We must form coalitions for change, often with partners well beyond the precincts of officialdom."[33] Reflecting this development, John Rawls envisions a more explicit role for civil society as he writes: "...it may turn out that there will be many different kinds of organizations subject to the judgment of the Law of Peoples and charged with regulating cooperation among them and meeting certain recognized duties."[34]

6. THE CIVIL SOCIETY PERIOD *(begins circa 1975)*

The third period of international law — that of civil society — captures emerging patterns of behavior in international relations. It focuses on the movement away from an emphasis on state values to a growing concern for human values.[35] Louis Henkin wrote:

> State autonomy remains a powerful value, but the distinction between state and human values continues to converge. The right of a state "to be let alone" subsumes the rights of its inhabitants to be let alone, to maintain their traditions and culture, as well as their ways of life.[36]

Table 3 shows the growth in multilateral treaty activity in the areas of human rights and more broadly in human welfare. (Human welfare includes items like health and food safety that do not fall directly under human rights and are included in the table as "Other Human Welfare.") Although increasing in numbers, multilateral treaties that address human rights and human welfare still generally account for less than 15% of overall multilateral treaty activity.

Table 3:
Multilateral Treaties
and Human Welfare by Period
1648-1995

Time Period	Total # of Treaties	Breakdown Number	Percent of Total
1648-1750	86	0	
1751-1850	100	Human rights: 13	13%
1851-1899	338	Human rights: 5	1%
		Other human welfare: 6	2%
1900-1925	663	Human rights: 50	8%
		Other human welfare: 18	3%
1926-1950	1183	Human rights: 119	10%
		Other human welfare: 25	2%
1951-1975	2047	Human rights: 119	6%
		Other human welfare: 39	2%
1976-1995	1619	Human rights: 86	5%
		Other human welfare: 25	2%

Power today is not only in the hands of 189 states and governments and the international institutions they have created, but also in those of private entities — multinational corporations, networks of individuals, and nongovernmental organizations (NGOs).

The burgeoning influence of nongovernmental organizations has generated a rich literature. Although the character of their long-term influence is not fully understood, there seems little disagreement that nongovernmental organizations are now a permanent feature of the international political landscape. Table 4 shows that the increase in the number of both IGOs and NGOs in the 20th century is impressive, but with a much more dramatic increase in the number of NGOs.

TABLE 4:
NUMBER OF IGOs AND NGOs BY
SELECTED YEARS

Year	Number of IGOs	Number of NGOs
1909	37	176
1951	123	832
1972	280	2173
1984	365	4615

David Held, *Political Theory and the Modern State: Essays on State, Power, and Democracy* (Stanford: Stanford University Press, 1989), p. 232.

Fewer than 300 NGOs were represented at the 1972 UN Environment Conference in Stockholm. At the 1992 environment conference in Rio, there were 1,400 NGOs attending the parallel NGO forum. In the area of human rights, at the 1993 UN World Human Rights Conference in Vienna, 248 NGOs were registered with 593 participants. At the Mexico City UN Women's Conference in 1975, 6,000 people attended the NGO forum. In 1985, there were 13,500 individuals registered for the Nairobi UN Women's Conference. And at the 1995 UN Women's Conference in Beijing, over 300,000 individuals attended.[37]

The NGO "cottage industry" has grown to such an extent that an intergovernmental gathering can be overshadowed by the activities of NGOs. NGOs increasingly have their own programs and activities. But their presence has created an additional source of political pressure that, if linked to other issues or to state sponsors, can develop into a potent political force. The prominence of women's issues on the international agenda today and the adoption of treaties like the Landmines Convention and the Statute for an International Criminal Court, are examples of strategic NGO-state alliances that resulted in highly effective political lobbying.[38]

One study of NGO influence at world conferences concluded that: "[t]heir importance resides in their role as monitors of governments perceived as unlikely or unable to resolve global problems."[39] Another observer of UN conference activity wrote that: "The expertise and experience of NGOs are invaluable inputs in decisionmaking processes, and UN conferences have significantly helped legitimize the participation of civil society in international arenas."[40] The ongoing work of NGOs will depend somewhat on the opportunities states and state institutions (including intergovernmental conferences) provide for direct or parallel activities from NGOs and how able NGOs are to seize these opportunities or to create additional ones. The 1999 demonstrations in Seattle during the World Trade Organization summit and subsequent protests during economic summits are examples of efforts — not all successful — to create new opportunities. NGOs have demonstrated their capacities as political forces and information resources and now draw on a growing coterie of individuals experienced in the related functions of international diplomacy and communication at high profile venues.

Voluntary networks have also demonstrated their power to influence states in the monitoring of state conduct in the treatment of their own citizens. *"Principled issue networks,"* as agents for change in state behavior and even in international standards, are a force for social change that appear to have emerged from the increased level of private transnational activity. Made possible through resources provided by foundations, spurred on by the commitment of individuals, and held together by new technologies, these transnationally linked organizations have had some notable achievements particularly in the protection of human rights.[41] The growing influence of the nongovernmental sector is seen through the consideration now being given in the UN to creating a people's assembly that would parallel the General Assembly as a regularly scheduled conclave, in contrast to the somewhat sporadic convening of world conferences or summits that have up to now been the principal focus for NGO activity.

These elements are sometimes grouped under the term "civil society," and they have been important curbs on state power — not only the power of states to do damage to other states, but also their power to harm individuals within their own territory. The events of fall 1998 surrounding Spain's request to the United Kingdom for the extradition of former Chilean President Augusto Pinochet are an example of this emerging area of legal and individual accountability for actions taken by serving government officials. The civil society image regards states as incapable of solving some problems, and as a contributing factor to other problems, whether environmental damage, weak economic and political development, or the abuse of individual human rights.

The technical character of many of the problems requiring international attention and the multi-sector cooperation needed to address them are also part of the explanation for the prominence and recognition of the power of the nongovernmental sector. Technology has also "broken governments' monopoly on the collection and management of large amounts of information."[42]

Events leading up to the signing of the convention to ban the use of anti-personnel landmines (Ottawa Convention, 1997) provided a recent example of the new power that individuals linked by technology, organized into a political network, and working in alliance with governments can wield.[43] The internet based campaign spearheaded by Jody Williams gained sufficient recognition for its efforts to win the Nobel Prize for Peace in 1997.

NGO involvement in the drafting of the Statute for the International Criminal Court and their role at the 1998 Rome intergovernmental conference on the ICC show another kind of NGO role. Here, the two year run-up to the Rome conference gave NGOs the opportunity to organize and to build relationships with UN secretariat staff and other key players in the drafting. This careful cultivation by the NGO coalition of opportunities for participation and influence paid off. At the end of the process, one NGO participant concluded that: "Governments and the team from the [UN] Office of Legal Affairs came to accept NGOs as indispensable consultants and worthwhile advocates."[44] That there may be as many ways for NGOs to be influential as there are issues does not diminish the general conclusion that they have become a political force on the international scene that is not likely to vanish.

Even two decades ago, the kind of *"people power"* generated by Helsinki Watch, Charter 77, Solidarity and other nongovernmental groups eventually created pressures for human rights and an end to the Cold War from within the Warsaw Pact countries themselves. Yet, while it seems clear that the public sector can no longer function effectively without the cooperation and participation of the private sector and the involvement of individual citizens, it remains true that the private sector cannot solve all problems without the infrastructure and coordination that states and international institutions provide. The 1975 Helsinki Final Act of the Conference on Security and Cooperation in Europe was, after all, an intergovernmental agreement that fostered an important "human dimension" through its system of follow-up conferences. The follow-up conferences also provided opportunities for NGOs seeking to liberalize the political institutions of the Warsaw Pact countries to gain political legitimacy and for their leaders to gain confidence in political activism and in the support of the international media for their efforts. The entire process fostered nothing less than a quiet and largely bloodless revolution.[45]

Evaluating the Civil Society Legacy

The civil society approach has much to commend in its open and broad based concept of participants in the international system. But it also has the potential of falling once again into Carr's utopian trap and moving law away from power. One particular area of danger is where NGOs push law beyond where an important power like the United States feels able to go, as the Peace Leagues of the 1930s demanded behavior from Britain that ultimately undermined their own goals. The lessons of the two earlier periods were twofold: that power needs to be recognized, and that long term commitments by key states are required for effective institution building and normative development. At the same time, the major powers need to realize that power alone is not sufficient to operate effectively, and that their interests require the structured frameworks that international cooperation can provide.

In other words, the operating and normative systems of international law must remain in alignment, so that the normative needs of the community can be met through existing but adaptable legal frameworks. What duties and obligations does the wider international community have with regard to individuals in their relationship with their own governing authorities? This is one dimension of the question the civil society poses for the operating system of international law today. Another question is the level of recognition to be given by states to the increasingly mobilized and politically vocal private associations active in the world today.

Both the operating and the normative systems of international law are facing these questions. How well international law will succeed in answering them depends on whether norms generated today meet the three-fold test of legal effectiveness: Are they clear and readily understood? Is there sufficient structure to put them into effect? And is there sufficient political consensus and political will to use them? Where the operating and normative do not appear well able to support each other, and where one of the three elements of effectiveness may not be in alignment, we are likely to face a situation where power and law may be too far apart to support the successful beginning of a new legal regime. These are the questions we face as we look into the issues of global governance for the 21st century.

7. CONCLUSION

Carr was right to remind us that law cannot always provide solutions. Where Carr fell short, however, was in his failure to appreciate the framework for political discourse that law provides. Such a framework, when accepted as legitimate by the holders of power — the major states in the system — enables these states to make collective progress toward finding common solutions for regional and global issues. The upcoming decades will give us ample opportunity to test whether our current framework can adapt to changing global issues and diffusion of power.

From the mechanics of state behavior and relations established in the voluntarist period, international law moved to restrain the power of states to wage war and to address a growing list of transnational issues in the institutionalist period. Although international institutions failed to eliminate war and conflict, they have shown a capacity to address an historically unprecedented agenda of international concerns. These concerns in turn have further changed the power structure in international law, producing the third period of civil society.

Although the voluntarist period seems to have promoted little beyond a state's authority to govern itself and its freedom to pursue international relations, a closer look reveals that self-preservation was a value that created enough commonality of interest to be regarded as forming the basis of some community.[46] The common interest went a step further to create the institutionalist period. These two periods continue to dwell uneasily together. Yet, the institutional structures and experiences of working together have provided the modes to address other areas of international concern that are now recognized - areas of environmental protection, economic well-being, and the protection of individual rights of citizens against the abuses of their own governments. This, in turn, has empowered the private sector to create additional political force through civil society.

The challenge now is for civil society to recognize the same lessons that international institutions had to learn in the early twentieth century. That is, to be effective requires working with what came before rather than rejecting it, even if that which came before is, in part the source of the problem. The demands of civil society have made identification of the norms and values of international law more complex, as the number of "authoritative decision-makers" and the number of subjects of international concern increase. This complexity puts greater reliance on a robust operating system to support appropriate political discourse and action.

Meeting the ongoing challenges of the future requires the ability to assess and to marshal resources for appropriate decision making. These include not only individuals skilled to address particular issues and resources, but also information to assess and to understand the problems being faced, and adequate political backing to understand the range of acceptable political behavior and the leadership required. Management of problems and the solution of problems should not be confused, but until the time is right for a solution, effective management, including the use of legal instruments, can be an important interim step.

I hope that considering these three periods has provided some indication of how international law has expanded the political space over the centuries to draw together elements of power, conflict, and interests into the international law-making and implementation process. From a passive reflection of power in the voluntarist period, to the interventionist effort to manage power in the institutionalist period, to the civil society period of diffused power, international law has evolved to respond to political change. In each case, it has created the space needed for fruitful interaction. These changes have not always come about peacefully or without cost and failure, but they have been effectively incorporated in the international system where the required elements of clarity, acceptability, and political consensus exist.

Throughout, we see that the effectiveness of international law depends on an accurate assessment of the power bases and political contexts in which legal standards and obligations must operate. Providing adequate space for political discourse and action is, I believe, key to global governance in the future. The large number of issues that characterize today's highly competitive and intensely political environment makes it hard to predict what the next crisis will be. As a result, only the availability of a ready and flexible framework with a growing and engaged body politic can provide a mode through which to define and to forge a solution. International law has demonstrated its ability to play its part in fostering this framework. I hope my presentation has helped explain how it has done so. I believe that our acceptance of the important contribution of international law as an operating system is essential towards generating a continuing and expanding global consensus on international norms.

Notes

1   Comprehensive Database of Multilateral Treaties (CDMT) developed by John King Gamble at The Behrend College, Pennsylvania State University (2000). This collection is based on materials published in Christian Wiktor, *Multilateral Treaty Calendar, 1648-1995* (Dordrecht: Martinus Nijhoff Publishers, 1998) and contains over 6,000 treaties. I appreciate the efforts of Jared Hawk, Teresa Bailey, and Aimee Peterson to adapt CDMT data for this lecture.

2   Edward Hallet Carr, *The Twenty Years' Crisis 1919-1939* (New York: Harper & Row, 1964), p. 180.

3   Charlotte Ku and Paul F. Diehl, "International Law as Operating and Normative Systems: An Overview," in *International Law: Classic and Contemporary Readings*, ed. Charlotte Ku and Paul F. Diehl (Boulder: Lynne Rienner, 1998), pp. 3-15.

4   See Hendrik Spruyt, *The Sovereign State and Its Competitors: An Analysis of Systems Change* (Princeton: Princeton University Press, 1994), p. 18.

5   See Bruce Bueno de Mesquita, "Popes, Kings, and Endogenous Institutions: The Concordat of Worms and the Origins of Sovereignty" in 2 *International Studies Review* (Summer 2000), pp. 93-118.

6   See James A. Caporaso, "Changes in the Westphalian Order: Territory, Public Authority, and Sovereignty," in 2 *International Studies Review* (Summer 2000), pp. 1-28. See also Leo Gross, "States as Organs of International Law and the Problem of Autointerpretation," in *Law and Politics in the World Community*, George A. Lipsky, ed. (Berkeley: University of California Press, 1953), pp. 59-88.

7   See Leo Gross, "The Peace of Westphalia, 1648-1948," 42 *American Journal of International Law* (1948), pp. 20-41.

8   As quoted in Leo Gross, "The Peace of Westphalia, 1648-1948," 42 *American Journal of International Law* (1948), p. 24.

9   See Charlotte Ku, "Catholicism, the Peace of Westphalia, and the Origins of Modern International law," 1 *The European Legacy* (1996), pp. 734-9.

10 Emphasis added. Permanent Court of International Justice, Series A/Judgments, no. 9, *The Case of the S.S. Lotus* (September 7, 1927).

11 See Louis Henkin, Chapter XV: Politics, Values and Functions at the Turn of the Century, in *International Law: Politics and Values* (Dordrecht: Martinus Nijhoff Publishers, 1995), pp. 279-96.

12 See Louis Henkin, Chapter XV: Politics, Values and Functions at the Turn of the Century, in *International Law: Politics and Values* (Dordrecht: Martinus Nijhoff Publishers, 1995), pp. 279-96.

13 Louis Henkin, "Away with the `S' Word," *ASIL Newsletter* (March-May 1993).

14 See Walter Mattli, "Sovereignty Bargains in Regional Integration," in 2 *International Studies Review* (Summer 2000), pp. 149-80.

15 Inis L. Claude, Jr., *Swords into Plowshares* (New York: Random House, 1984), p. 21.

16 Edward Hallet Carr, *The Twenty Years' Crisis 1919-1939* (New York: Harper & Row, 1964), p. 174.

17 Pitman B. Potter, "Article XIX of the Covenant of the League of Nations," *Geneva Studies* 12 (August 1943), p. 25.

18 See David Hunter Miller, *The Drafting of the Covenant*, volume 1 (New York: G.P. Putnam's Sons, 1928).

19 See Charlotte Ku, "Change and Stability in the International System: China Secures Revision of the Unequal Treaties," pp. 447-61, in *Essays in Honor of Wang Tieya*, ed. Ronald St. J. Macdonald (Martinus Nijhoff Publishers, 1993.)

20 Harold K. Jacobson, *Networks of Interdependence: International Organizations and the Global Political System*, 2nd edition (New York: Alfred A. Knopf, 1984), p. 349.

21 Harold K. Jacobson, *Networks of Interdependence: International Organizations and the Global Political System*, 2nd edition (New York: Alfred A. Knopf, 1984), p. 349.

22 Rosalyn Higgins, *Problems & Process: International Law and How We Use It* (Oxford: Clarendon Press, 1994), p. 113.

23 Oscar Schachter, " The UN Legal Order: An Overview," in *The United Nations and International Law*, ed. Christopher Joyner (Cambridge: Cambridge University Press, 1997), p. 3.

24 Jonathan I. Charney, "Universal International Law," 87 *American Journal of International Law* (October 1993), p. 551.

25 See Fanny Benedetti and John L. Washburn, "Drafting the International Criminal Court Treaty: Two Years to Rome and an Afterword on the Rome Diplomatic Conference," 3 *Global Governance* (1999), pp. 1-37.

26 Cheryl Shanks, Harold K. Jacobson, and Jeffrey H. Kaplan, "Inertia and change in the constellation of international governmental organizations, 1981-1992," 50 *International Organization* (Autumn 1996), p. 594.

27 Cheryl Shanks, Harold K. Jacobson, and Jeffrey H. Kaplan, "Inertia and change in the constellation of international governmental organizations, 1981-1992," 50 *International Organization* (Autumn 1996), p. 593.

28 Harold K. Jacobson, "International Institutions and System Transformation," *Annual Review of Political Science 2000*, p. 149.

29 International Court of Justice, *Advisory Opinion on the Reparation for Injuries Suffered in the Service of the United Nations* (11 April 1949), p. 9.

30 Anne-Marie Burley (Slaughter) and Walter Mattli, "Europe Before the Court: A Political Theory of Legal Integration," 47 *International Organization* (Winter 1993), p. 42.

31 European Court of Human Rights, *Lawless*, Series A/Judgments nos. 2 and 3 (7 April and 1 July 1961).

32 European Court of Human Rights, *Case relating to Certain Aspects of the Laws on the Use of Languages in Education in Belgium*, Series A/Judgment no. 6 (23 July 1958).

33 UN Secretary-General Kofi A. Annan, *"We the Peoples": The Role of the United Nations in the 21st Century* (New York: United Nations, 2000), p. 7.

34 John Rawls, *The Law of Peoples* (Cambridge: Harvard University Press, 1999), p. 36.

35 See Louis Henkin, Chapter XV: Politics, Values and Functions at the Turn of the Century, in *International Law: Politics and Values* (Dordrecht: Martinus Nijhoff Publishers, 1995), p. 284.

36 Louis Henkin, Chapter XV: Politics, Values and Functions at the Turn of the Century, in I*nternational Law: Politics and Values* (Dordrecht: Martinus Nijhoff Publishers, 1995), p. 284.

37 Ann Marie Clark, Elisabeth J. Friedman, Kathryn Hochstetler, "The Sovereign Limits of Global Civil Society," 51 *World Politics* (October 1998), p. 9.

38 Charlotte Ku (with John King Gamble), "International Law—New Actors and New Technologies: Center Stage for NGOs?" *Law and Policy in International Business*, Volume 31, No. 2, (Winter 2000), pp. 221-62.

39 Ann Marie Clark, Elisabeth J. Friedman, Kathryn Hochstetler, "The Sovereign Limits of Global Civil Society," 51 *World Politics* (October 1998), p. 21.

40 Jacques Fomerand, "UN Conferences: Media Events or Genuine Diplomacy?" 2 *Global Governance* (1996), p. 372.

41 Kathryn Sikkink, "Human Rights, Principled Issue-Networks, and Sovereignty in Latin America, " 47 *International Organization* (Summer 1993), pp. 411-41.

42 Jessica T. Mathews, "Power Shift," 76 *Foreign Affairs* (January/February 1997), p. 57.

43 See Stephen Greene, "A Campaign to Sweep Away Danger," 60 *Chronicle of Philanthropy* (20 October 1997). See also Richard Price, "Transnational Civil Society Targets Land Mines," 52 *International Organization* (Summer 1998), pp. 613-44.

44 Fanny Benedetti and John L. Washburn, "Drafting the International Criminal Court Treaty: Two Years to Rome and an Afterword on the Rome Diplomatic Conference," 3 *Global Governance* (1999), p. 25.

45 See Thomas Buergenthal, "CSCE Human Dimension: The Birth of a System," in *Collected Course of the Academy of European Law* (1992).

46 See, for example, Hedley Bull, "The Grotian Conception of International Society," in *Diplomatic Investigations*, ed. Herbert Butterfield and Martin Wight. (London: 1966).